# COUCHING
## decorative laid thread embroidery

# COUCHING
## decorative laid thread embroidery

Gloria Ramsey

B T Batsford Limited
London

Filmset by Servis Filmsetting Limited, Manchester

Printed in Great Britain by
The Anchor Press, Tiptree, Essex
for the publishers
B T Batsford Limited
4 Fitzhardinge Street
London W1H 0AH

# Contents

# Acknowledgment

I would like to thank Gerry Broughton for his excellent photography, Millicent Wright for the loan of her work and Messrs B. T. Batsford Ltd for the illustrations on pages 22, 24 and 25 from *Metal Thread Embroidery* by Barbara Dawson, pages 20 and 21 from *Ecclesiastical Embroidery* by Beryl Dean, page 26 from *Design in Embroidery* by Kathleen Whyte and page 76 from *Canvas Embroidery* by Diana Springall.

My grateful thanks are also due to Miss Thelma Nye of B. T. Batsford Ltd for her help and encouragement and to my husband, David, for his unfailing kindness and constant understanding.

Metal, lace, ribbon, strips of nylon, felt
and leather couched onto canvas

# Introduction

Couching is holding down a line of thread by means of another thread. The laid, or held down, thread is called the couched thread, whilst the thread which holds it down is called the couching thread. Laid work is a close relative of couching; it is a method of filling whole areas with couched threads which lie so closely together that no ground fabric is visible between.

Couching is basically a linear treatment, but traditionally it was used to fill solid areas, cover the edges of appliqué and define outlines. Couching may form open fillings, add interest and texture to background treatment, or become an integral part of the design.

The most important aspect of couching is the choice of threads. The couched thread is generally thicker than the couching thread but for decorative purposes, there is no reason why the reverse should not apply. Exciting effects may be gained by experiment. Is the couched thread to be completely visible or is it to be decorated by the couching thread? The couching thread may be unobtrusive or it may command attention because of its colour, texture or decorative effect.

Besides the embroidery threads in common use, anything which is flexible enough can be used as a couching thread, such as strings and twines, cords, crochet, knitting and rug wools, weaving yarns and mixtures, sewing threads, metal threads, raffene, synthetic fibres, thongs and laces, strips of fabric, nets and leather; experimentation is the key word.

Strips of nylon fabric couched with perle

Couched threads as fillings

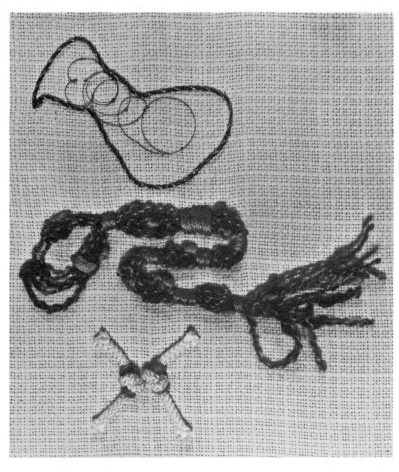

Metal thread, fine wire, courtelle knitting yarn and nylon tent rope as couched threads

Knitting wools, nylon fibre and vegetable netting as couched threads

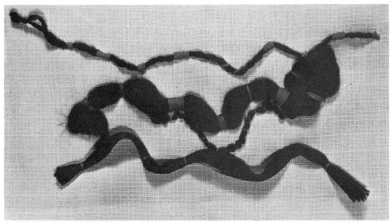

13

Knitting wools and perlita couched with
stranded silk

# Couching with metal threads

Couching probably originated as a method of sewing down gold thread in the most economical manner, and at the same time overcoming the difficulty of drawing the thread down through the fabric. Gold threads were used extensively on ecclesiastical vestments and ceremonial robes.

In the mediaeval type of underside couching two needles were used; one laid the thread on the surface, the other – threaded with linen – came up through the surface, couched the surface thread and returned by the same hole to the reverse side of the fabric, pulling the thread with it, which explains its French name *point rentre et retire*. This interlocking of the two threads is a similar process to that of the modern sewing machine when using a normal straight stitch.

The mediaeval method of couching also gave a more flexible surface, which was of great advantage in vestments; it was hardwearing too. It was in use throughout Europe by the end of the twelfth century. Underside couching was characteristic of the *Opus Anglicanum* period, but surface couching continued to be practised elsewhere and eventually superseded underside couching.

Another traditional method was Bokhara couching; here the couching and the couched thread are one and the same. The couching stitches must be fairly close together if a large surface area is to be covered. The stitches should be firm. Roumanian couching employs the same method as Bokhara but the couching stitches are longer in this case, and slanting across the laid thread; they should be much looser than Bokhara.

Laidwork was extensively used in seventeenth century Italian ecclesiastical embroidery though its origins are much earlier. Laid threads completely cover the ground fabric, then patterns are made on this by couching stitches or further threads worked into decorative patterns, which are in turn couched down. These may give a rich texture or a flat surface to contrast perhaps with a nearby rich area. Shading or irregular patches of colour can also be introduced by areas of laidwork.

Mediaeval method of couching: the dotted
line is the ground fabric, the thick upper
line is the gold thread which the linen
thread underneath the fabric is couching

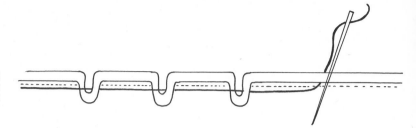

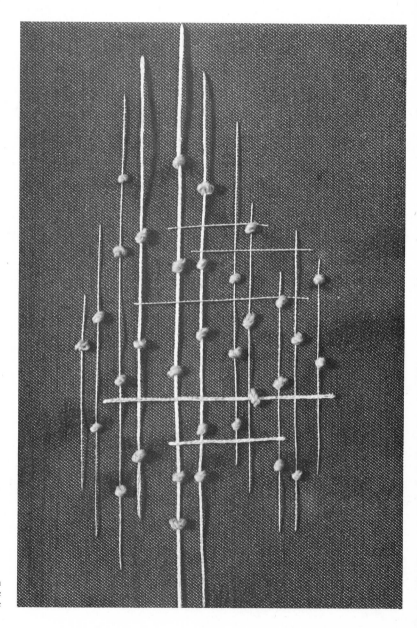

Loosely-laid silk thread couched down with
loose wool loops; an idea derived from the
reverse side of underside couching technique

16

Bokhara couching uses one thread only for both the couching and the couched line. The couching stitches may form patterns if required

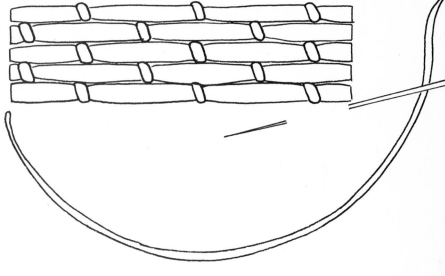

Roumanian couching is similar to Bokhara couching in that it uses only one thread for both the couching and the couched line. The couching stitch, however, is much looser and covers more of the couched line than Bokhara couching

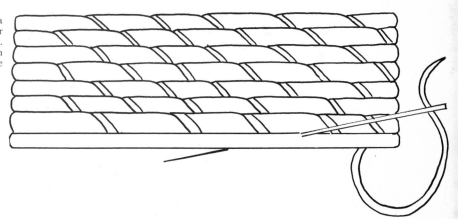

The design and execution of ecclesiastical embroidery involves many skills; a feeling for contemporary ideas which will translate into a satisfying design, an awareness of the interaction of fabrics, threads, colours and the effect these should have in the place in which they will be seen. When metal threads are to be used, consideration of the surrounding surfaces is necessary; a shiny ground would not show the metal threads to advantage but a matt surface obviously would.

Laidwork motif in silk over laid-tapiesserie
wool

Today the choice of metal threads is wide; there are the pure metal varieties as well as the synthetic types of gold, silver and alloys. Jap gold and silver threads and cords are used because the best quality (Admiralty or Government standard $2\frac{1}{2}/90$) is least likely to tarnish. Medium quality is gold $1\frac{1}{2}/50$ and the cheapest quality is called gilt – this is more likely to tarnish with time.

This choice has in turn led to a broader interpretation of metal thread work. Some of the more flexible threads such as lurex and crochet twist in gold, silver and coloured tones can be used in conjunction with the domestic sewing machine to cover large areas quickly, so allowing the more expensive metal threads to be used sparingly, as the focal point of the design. A specialized book should be consulted before attempting formal gold work, but generally the metal threads are worked on the surface – unlike ordinary sewing threads – as entry into the fabric too frequently would weaken it; a frame is essential. Gold threads are usually couched two at a time with stitches of Maltese silk or horse-tail; these couching stitches are set at right angles to the couched thread and cover the width without pulling the couched thread out of shape. The ends of the metal threads are always pulled from the right side down to the underside of the fabric.

The play of light on metal thread embroidery gives it a lustrous 3-D quality; this may be achieved by couching over string, felt and cardboard and also by the addition of gold and silver leathers as well as jewels and beads.

The couching of gold thread and fine silk particularly lends itself to patterning by placing the couching stitches carefully. There are many traditional patterns such as Lattice, Waved and Italian. Other patterns can be made by couching threads over an area already covered by laid and couched threads.

Light and dark areas can be indicated in flat work by placing the couching stitches close together for darker areas and far apart for lighter areas. Shapes are made by couching with close stitches in appropriate colours whilst the background is couched in widely spaced stitches in a matching colour. This method of work is called *or nue*.

(a) St Peter – an example of laid work in silk
(b) Side panel of a triptych worked in *or nue*, mainly in jade greens, greys and orange, on a dark blue ground From *Ecclesiastical Embroidery* by *Beryl Dean*

(b)

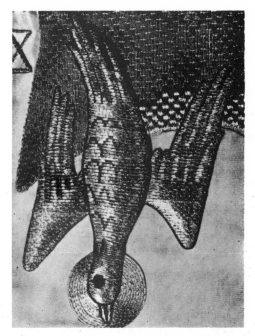

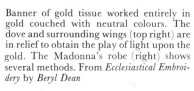

Banner of gold tissue worked entirely in
gold couched with neutral colours. The
dove and surrounding wings (top right) are
in relief to obtain the play of light upon the
gold. The Madonna's robe (right) shows
several methods. From *Ecclesiastical Embroidery* by *Beryl Dean*

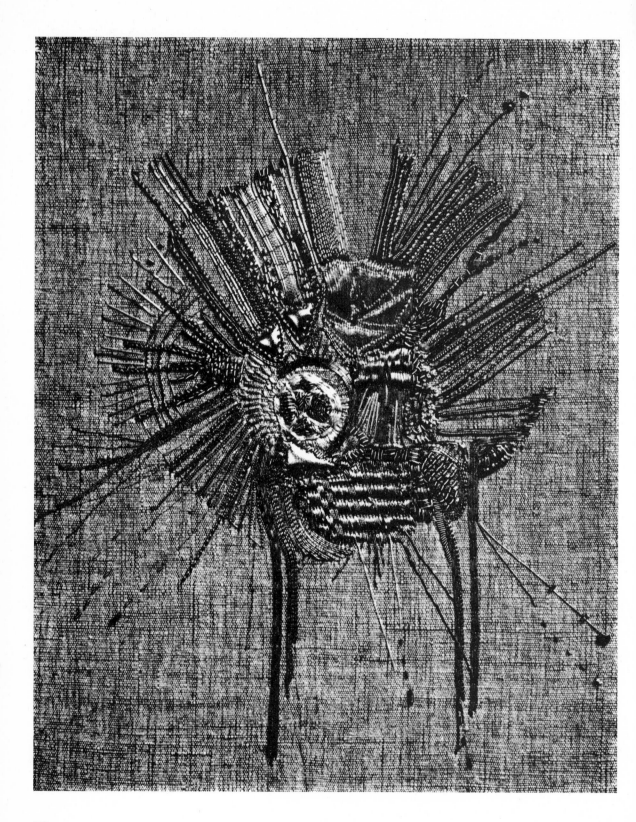

Modern goldwork using couched metal threads on a rough matt gold and white woven furnishing textile. From *Metal Thread Embroidery* by *Barbara Dawson*. **Adrienne Hamilton**

Modern goldwork on magenta satin with velvet. **Millicent Wright**

A design inspired by engineering and, except for the areas of gold kid, worked entirely in couche rentre, or underside couching. The metal thread is a fine, pliable machine thread sewn down with maltese silk, with a central area of silk mixed with gold. The smaller photographs on page 25 show the back of the work with small loops of gold and silk thread drawn through by the couching silk. From *Metal Thread Embroidery* by *Barbara Dawson*. **Judith Summers**

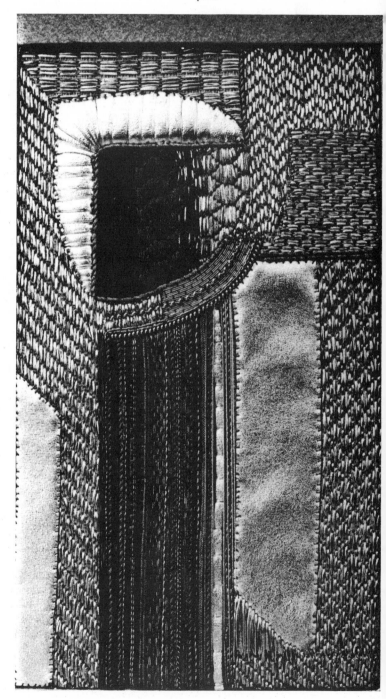

OPPOSITE
*Plate 2*   Wall panel of applied fabrics and
nets with various wools and threads couched
by machine. Leaf stitch couching added by
hand

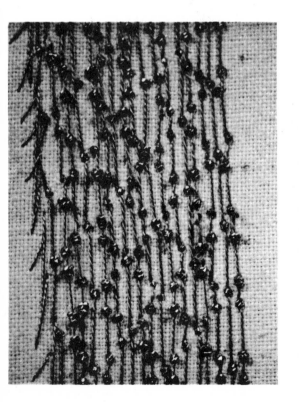

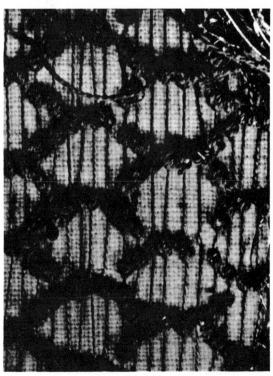

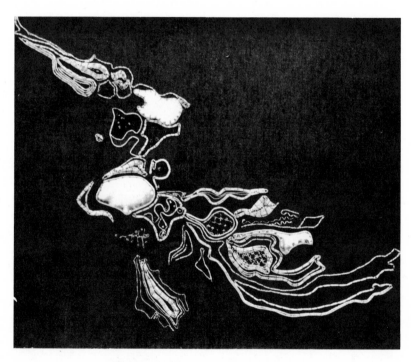

Silver embroidery on green. From *Design in Embroidery* by *Kathleen Whyte*. **Catriona Leslie**

# Couching with flat stitches

Flat stitches are the largest group of stitches and they are the simplest group to execute. Traditionally they are worked very evenly but a freer approach to them reveals exciting possibilities.

Taking the emerging couching thread across the couched thread and returning into the ground fabric is the simplest form of flat stitch but variety can be added by grouping or patterning the couching stitches. Flat stitches, which are usually worked in blocks, may still be used for couching simply by placing the blocks of stitchery in proportion to the couched thread.

Stem stitch makes an angular line by lengthening each individual stitch. This may then be couched down by another stitch.

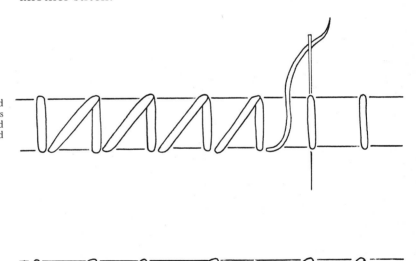

snian or double running stitch is worked two stages. It is suitable for dress broidery when worked closely and nly. The lower version is much freer and re versatile

27

Chevron stitch covers the couched thread
heavily

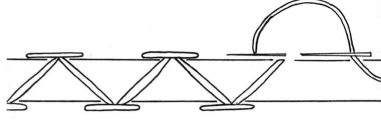

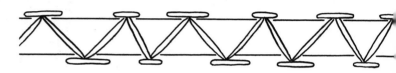

Satin stitch may be worked in any number
of patterns as a couching stitch

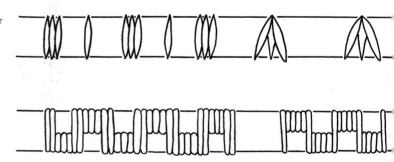

Stem stitch as a couched line

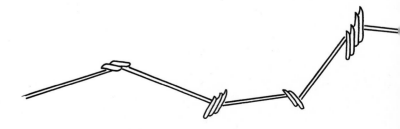

urface satin stitch differs from ordinary
tin stitch in that the needle picks up a
all piece of fabric at each side of the laid
uched thread without passing round,
derneath and up

tin stitch couching down a stem stitch
uched line

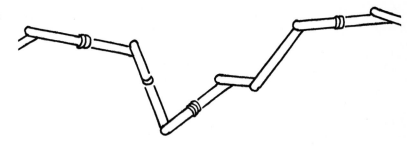

eaf stitch covers the couched thread
eavily

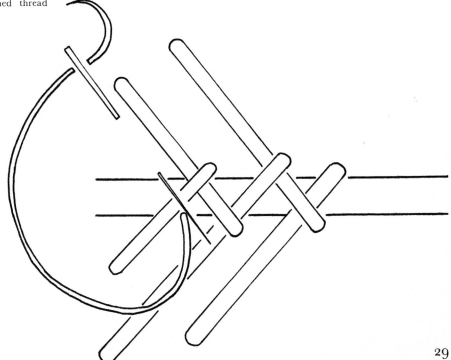

Open fishbone stitch covers the couched thread very heavily

Flat stitch can be worked on wide, flat couched threads such as ribbon, bias binding and raffene

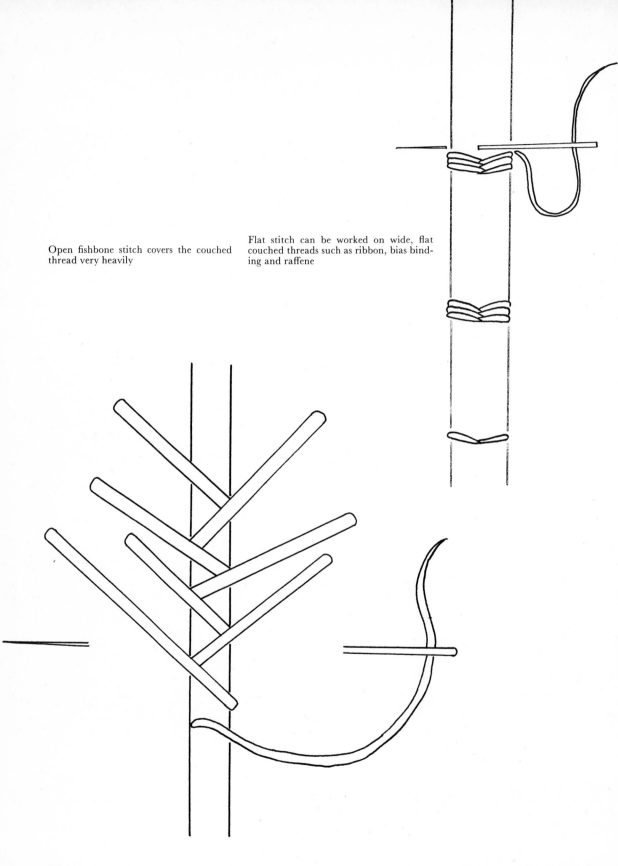

Straight stitch and uneven cross stitch
couching a variety of threads

Detail from colour plate 1 showing herringbone stitch couching thick wool
chain couching a variety of threads
Straight stitch, back stitch and detached

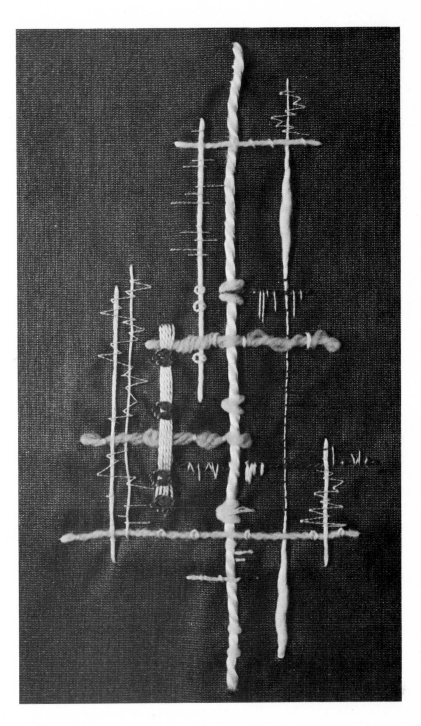

33

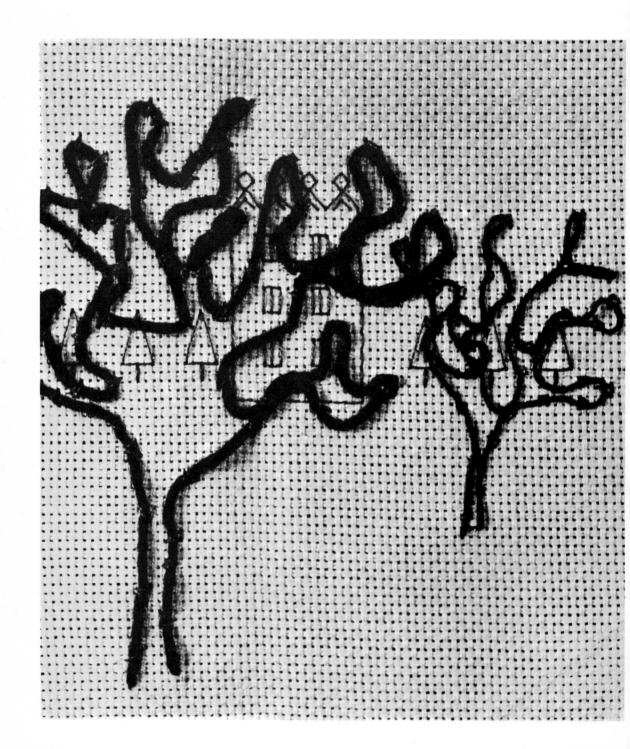

34

Left: Back-stitched triangles couching heavy threads over a blackwork background

Chevron stitch and long-armed cross stitch couching over wool

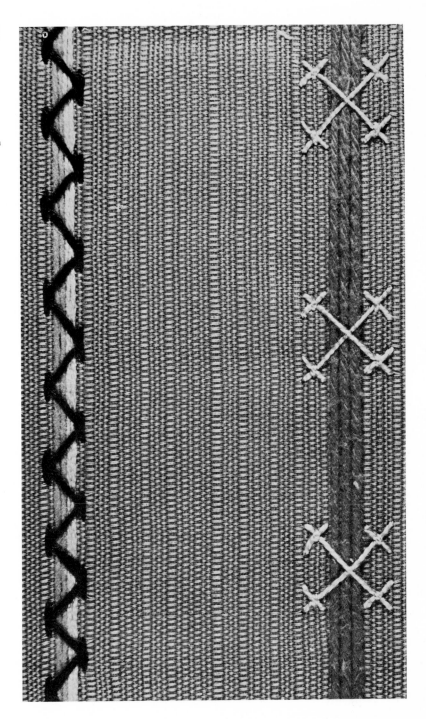

Couching stitch in Coton-à-broder over soft wool

Flat stitch couching a thick wool

Plaited wools, perlita and stranded silk couched down with a slanting couching stitch in free and regular groupings

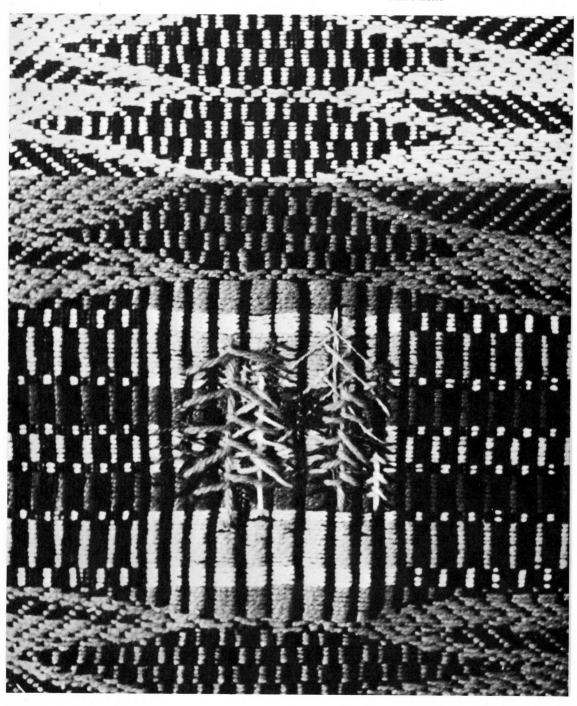

Slanting couching stitch over wools on a
chain stitch motif. **Millicent Wright**

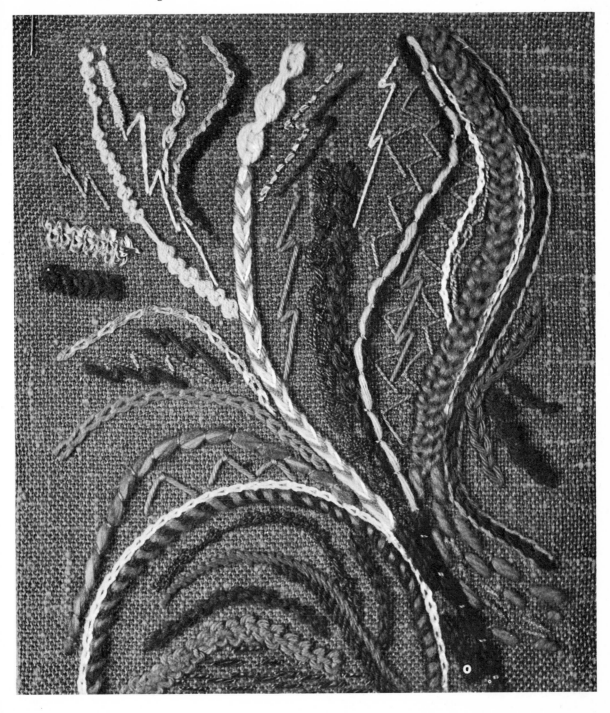

Bosnian stitch couching (from left to right)
vegetable netting, strip of organdie, terry
towelling, crochet twist, wool and perlita

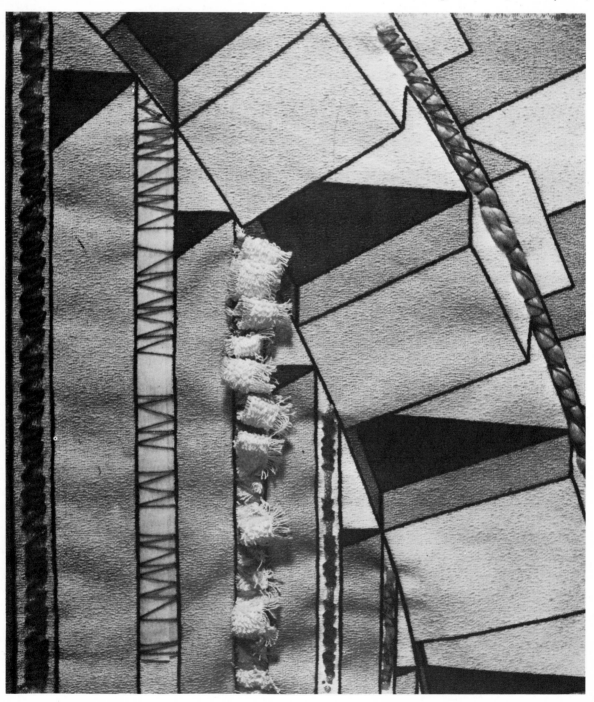

Stem stitch as a couched line in itself with
other threads couched by irregular blocks
of satin stitch

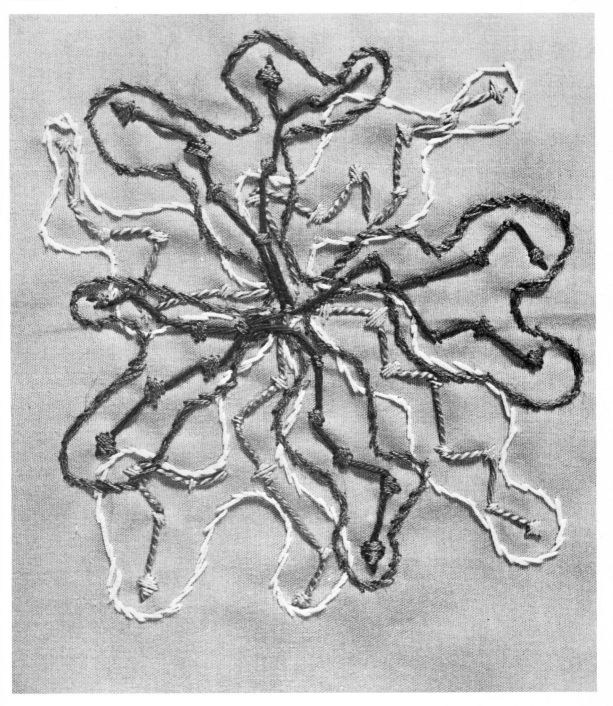

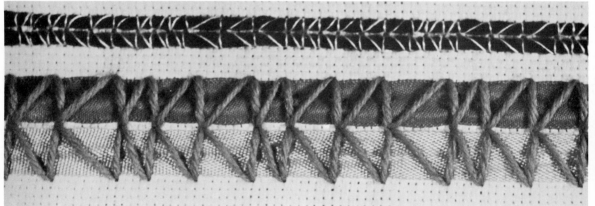

Triangle stitch couching ribbon             Triangle stitch couching perlita and ribbon

# Couching with looped stitches

Most looped stitches are varieties of buttonhole. There is evidence of the use of buttonhole stitch in Elizabethan dress embroidery; in some cases it was used to couch down gold and silk threads.

Infinite variety in couching stitches is available with looped stitches. The placing of the uprights in buttonhole is open to choice as is the spacing between each stitch. Buttonhole may also be worked as a couched line in its own right. Fly and feather stitch may also be treated thus.

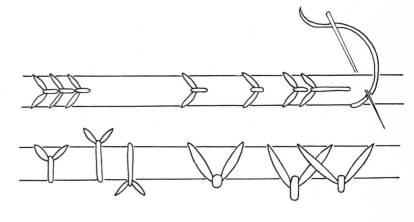

Fly stitch may be detached or joined, worked parallel or at right angles to the couched thread, or it may be worked as a couched line in itself

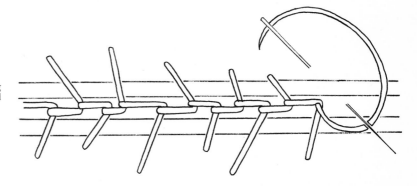

Long armed feather stitch shown couching two parallel threads. It could also be used down the centre of a very broad thread

Feather stitch is very versatile. It can be worked closely or spaced, evenly or freely, continuously or in blocks

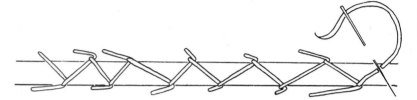

Open Cretan stitch used as a loose couching stitch

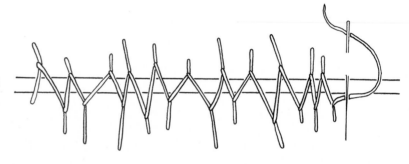

Sword stitch is an unusual asymmetric stitch which couches lightly; it is best used on thick couched threads

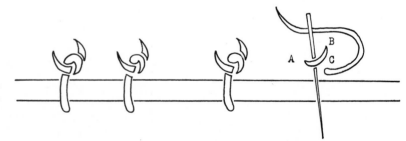

Buttonhole stitch as a couched line

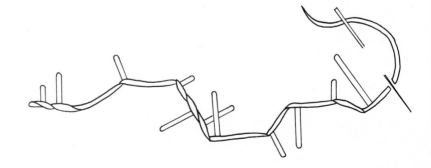

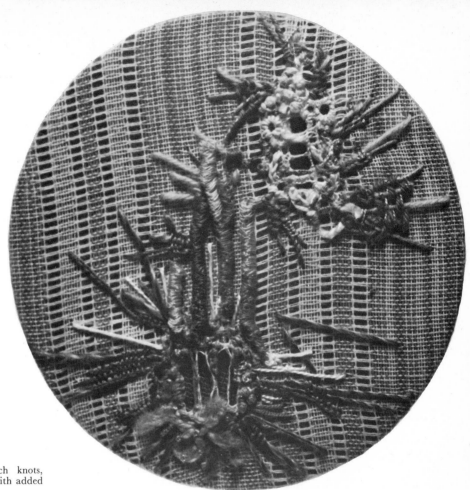

Buttonhole, satin stitch, french knots, couching a variety of threads with added needleweaving

Single and double feather stitch couching a cinnamoid spiral shape

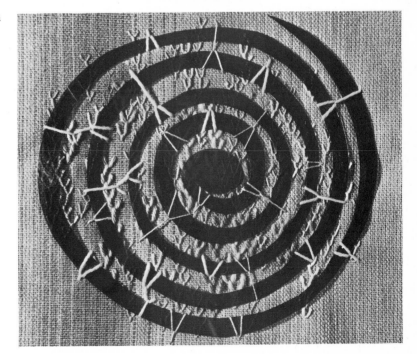

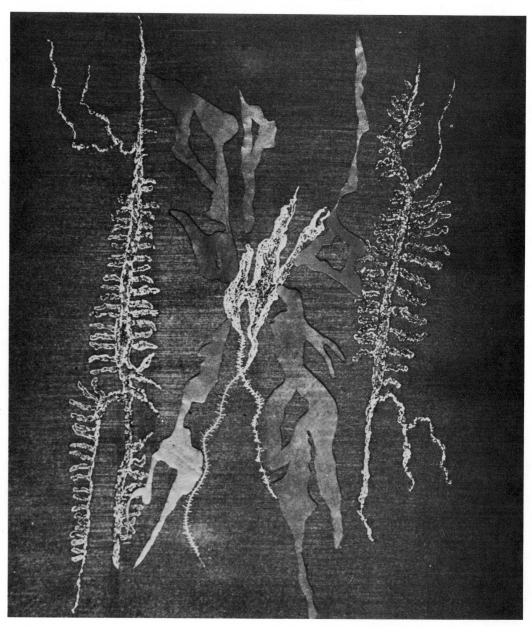

Detail from the previous figure showing fly
stitch couching fine thread

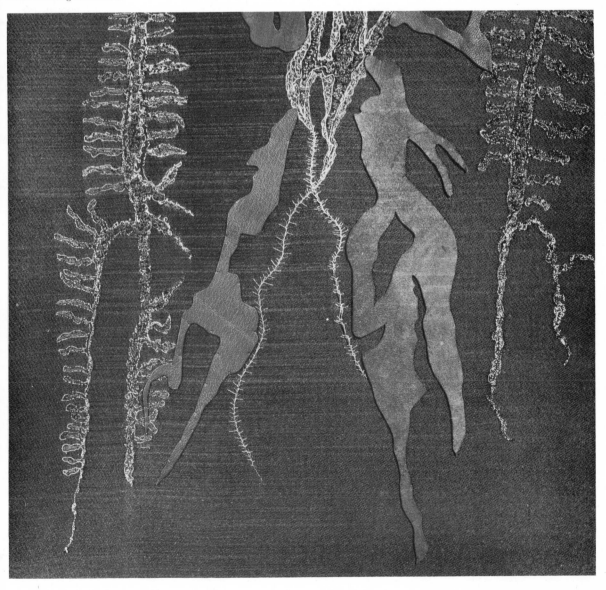

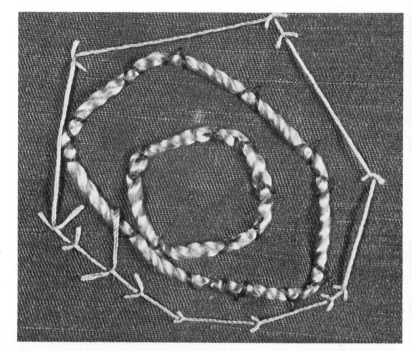

Fly stitch as a couched line around perlita thread couched with fly stitch

Cretan stitch couching thick wool and woven cellophane

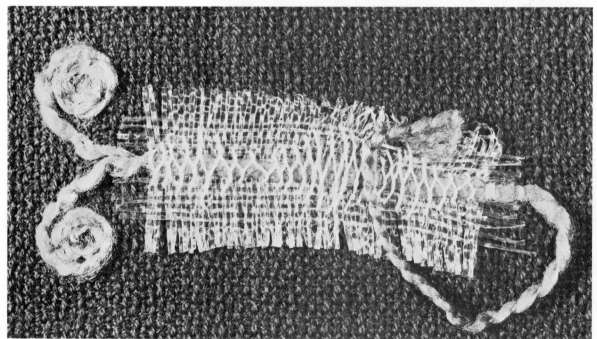

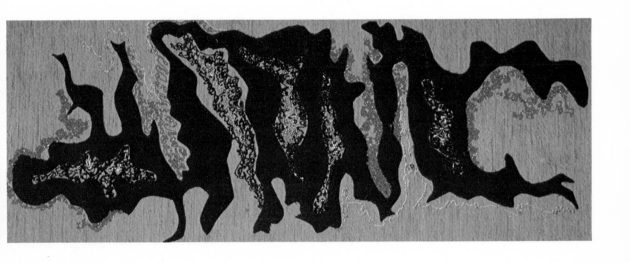

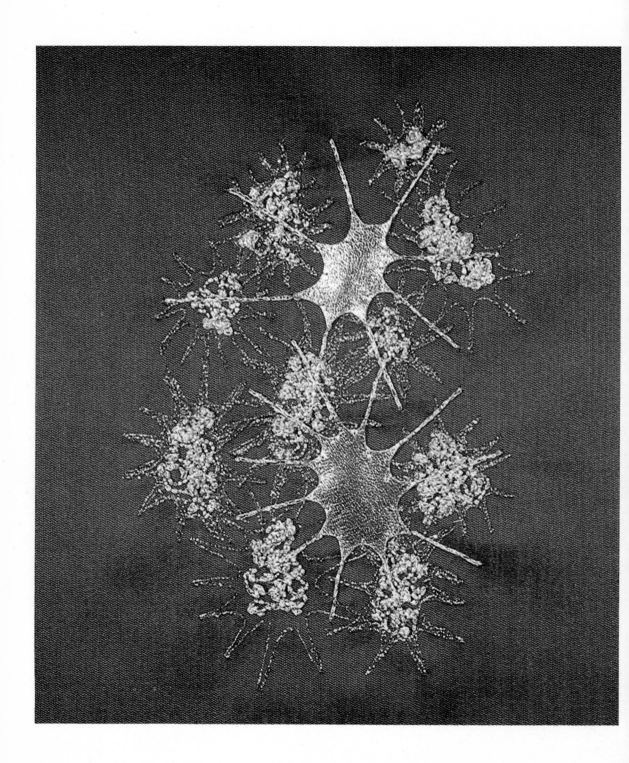

*Plate 4*   The centres were worked from the
back in silver crochet twist by loosening the
tension screw on the bobbin case, removing
the presser foot and lowering the feed
teeth. The outer shapes around them are in
lurex thread worked from the front with the
presser foot removed and a normal tension
on the bobbin case screw. The silver kid
shapes were added by hand

Detached fly stitch couching fine threads
and net on a batik fabric

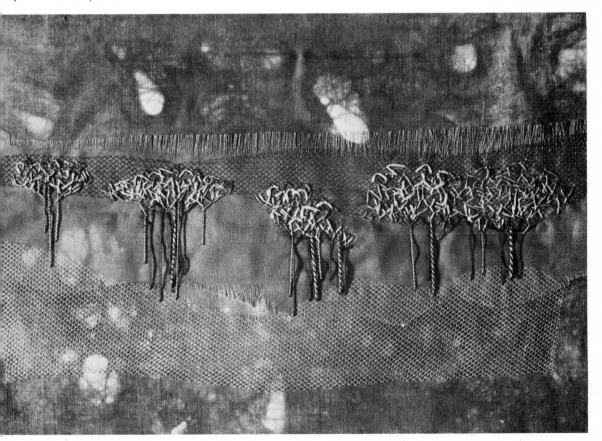

Sword stitch couching plaited wool     Buttonhole stitch couching heavy cord

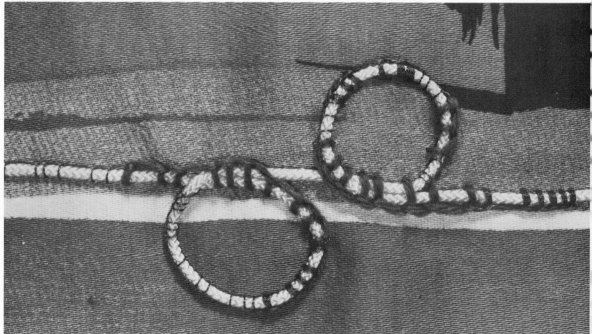

Up and down buttonhole stitch couching
ribbon and strips of nylon

Up and down buttonhole stitch in patterns
over various wools

# Couching with chained stitches

Most of the silk work of English mediaeval ecclesiastical embroidery was carried out in chain stitch for it is equally good for fillings and lines. Split stitch or chain was used for shading on features and drapery in *Opus Anglicanum*.

Chain as a couching stitch tends to cover much of the couched thread; detached chain is an exception. Open chain gives a firm effect but needs to be in a thin thread if the couched thread is to be shown to advantage.

Chain stitch in a fine but firm thread makes an interesting couched line in itself.

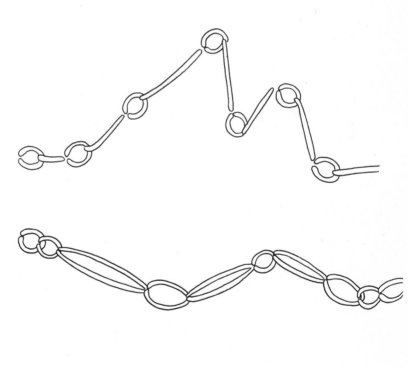

Chain stitch as a couched line

Detached chain stitch as a couching stitch

53

Detached chain couching soft cotton and silk

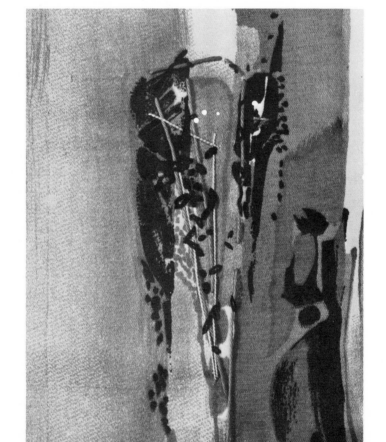

Motif showing a variety of stitches and
techniques. Threads at top left are couched
with detached chain. **Millicent Wright**

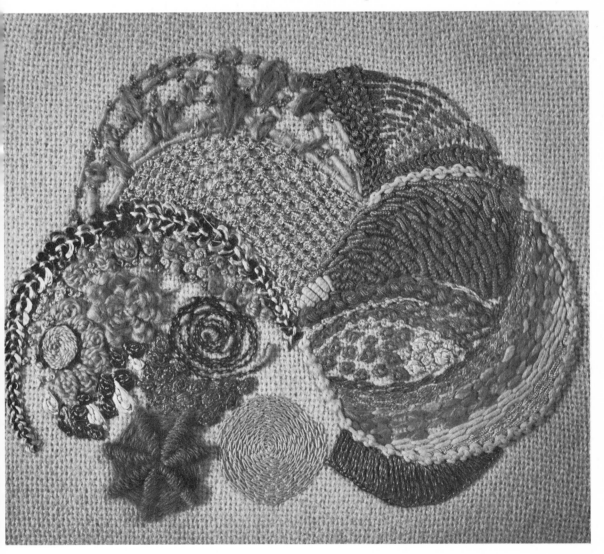

Open chain and coral knot stitch couching
a variety of threads

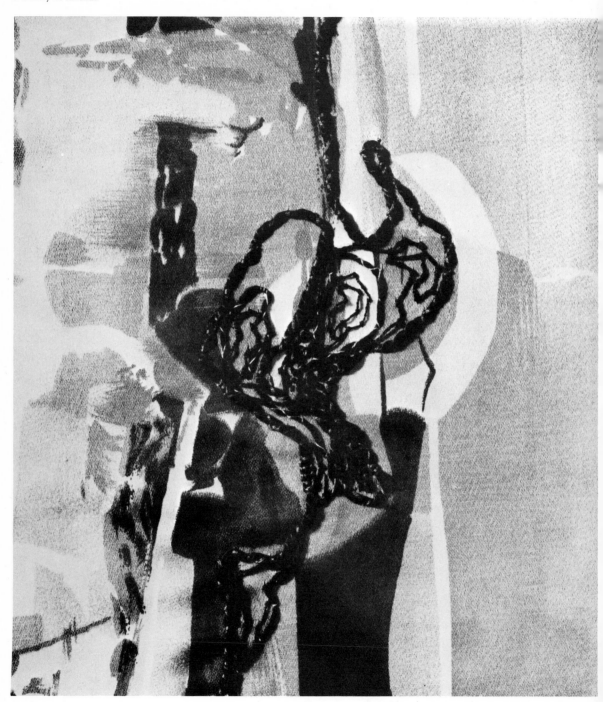

Cockerel in fly and feather stitch with a
variety of threads couched in detached
chain. **Millicent Wright**

Thick and thin threads couched with open chain, herringbone, cross stitch, buttonhole and detached chain. **Millicent Wright**

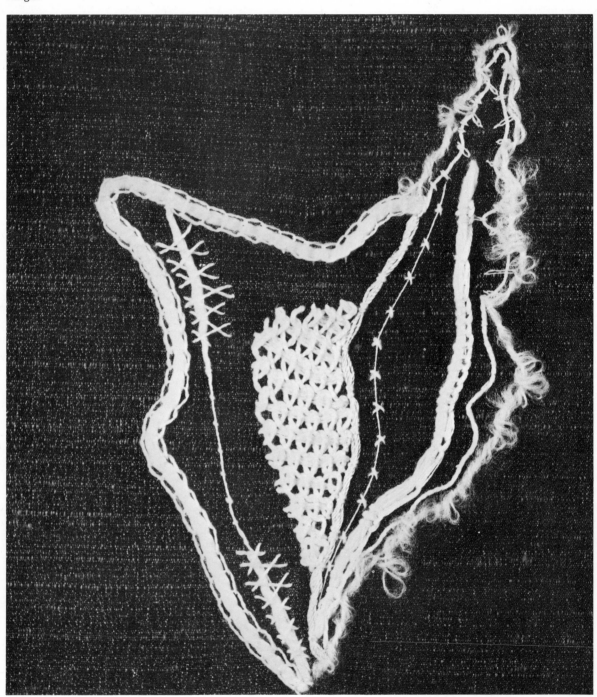

# Couching with knotted stitches

Knotted stitches make an interesting contrast to smooth threads and fabrics. Flat threads such as raffene may be couched by french knots but care should be taken over the placing of these; too few can look 'spotty' whilst too many can look clumsy.

Sorbello stitch is a useful couching stitch which adds interest to the couched line.

Sorbello stitch couches the thread lightly. The legs may be lengthened as required

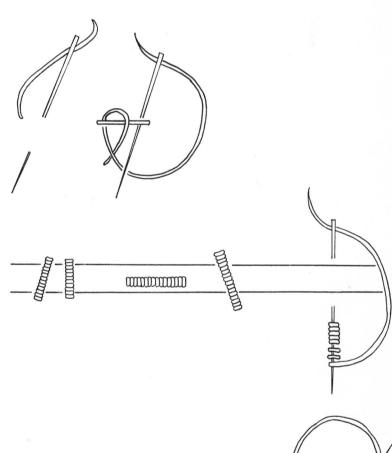

Bullion knots couching a thick couched thread

Coral stitch as a couched line

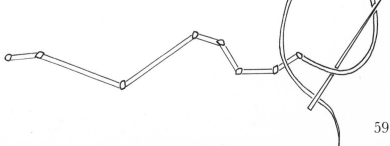

French knot stitch as a couched line. It can
also be used to couch flat threads

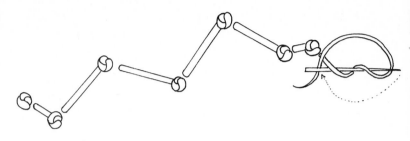

Double knot stitch as a couched line

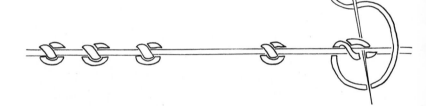

Danish knot stitch is a heavy stitch which
can be used to couch firm, thick threads.
It looks well as a couched line in itself

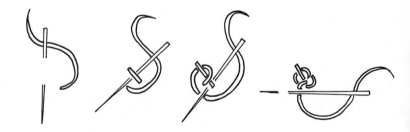

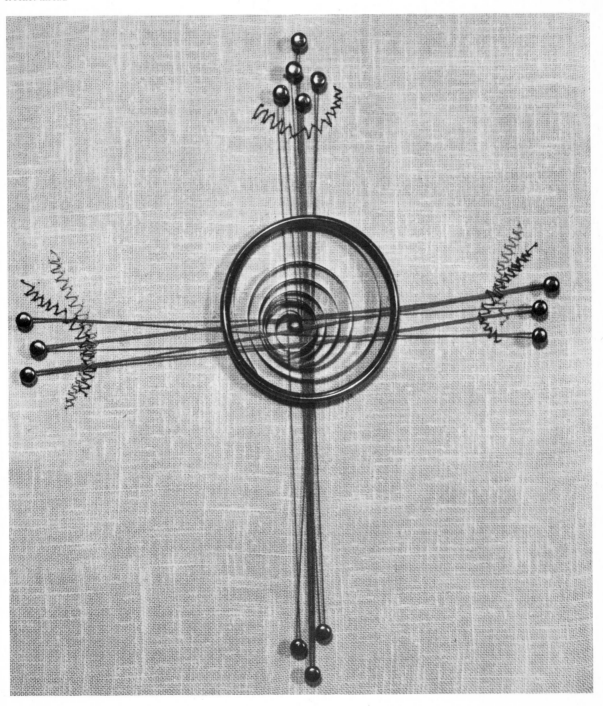

Bullion and french knots couching raffene
with double knot around centre as a
couched line stitch. Outer hank of wool
held down by coral stitch

Sorbello stitch couching thick wool and
string

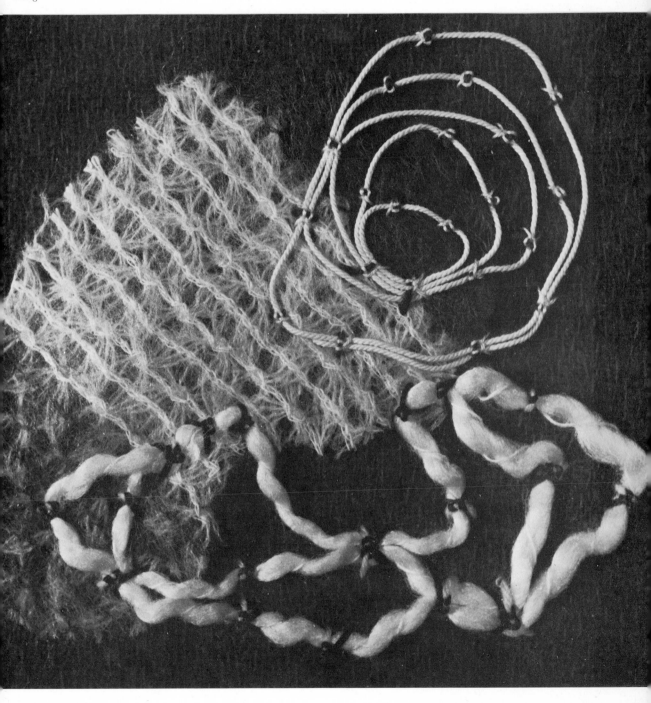

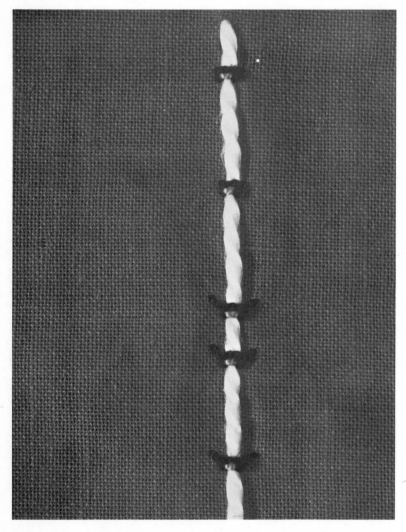

# Couching with composite stitches

Composite stitches usually consist of two or more stitches; one makes the foundation and subsequent stitches are added to it, either by lacing or entwining. This means that much of the couched thread is covered by the couching stitch, so spaces should be left between blocks of couching to show the couched thread to advantage.

Lock stitch is versatile, as the upright bars may be irregularly spaced to allow the couched thread to show.

Lock stitch – much improvisation is possible with the lacing thread over the foundation of straight stitches

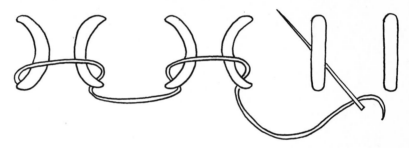

Raised chain band couches heavily, but it can be detached or spaced so that the couched thread is seen to advantage

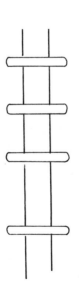
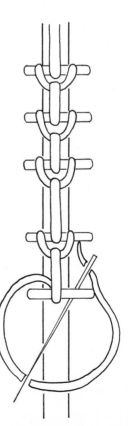

Lurex and fine threads couched down by
wheels and clock parts

Detail of colour plate 1, showing thick
wools couched with lock stitch and herringbone

Raised chain band couching various threads

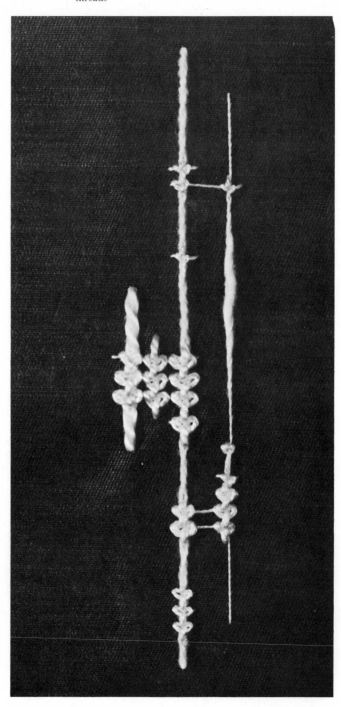

Detail from work showing thick wools
couched by interlaced band

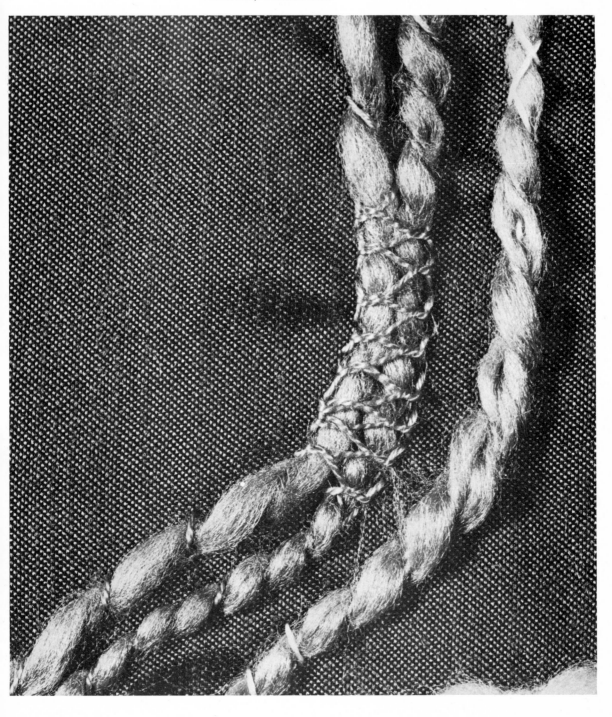

Interlaced band couching (from left to right) raffene, vegetable netting and wool

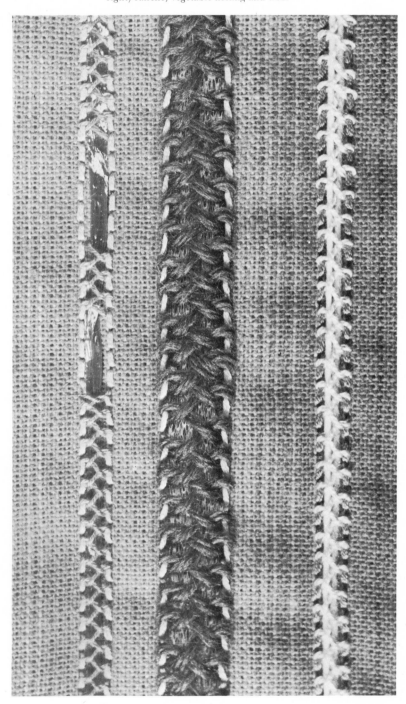

Lock stitch couching wool, vegetable netting and perlita

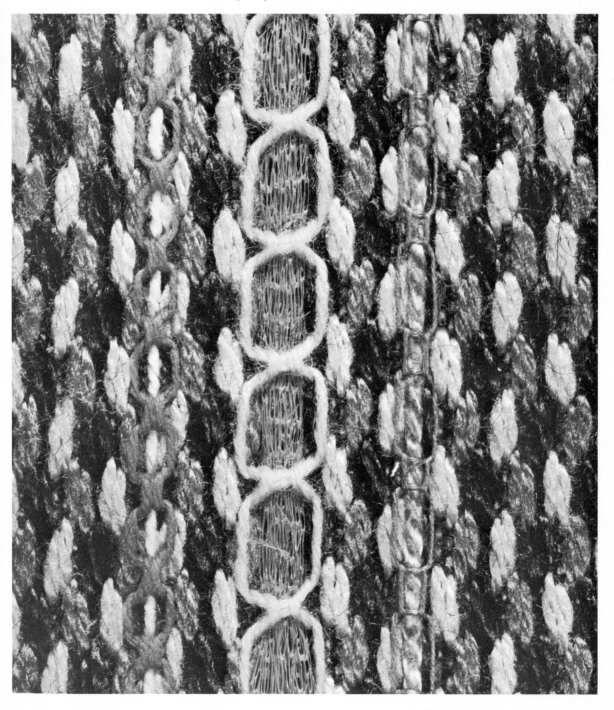

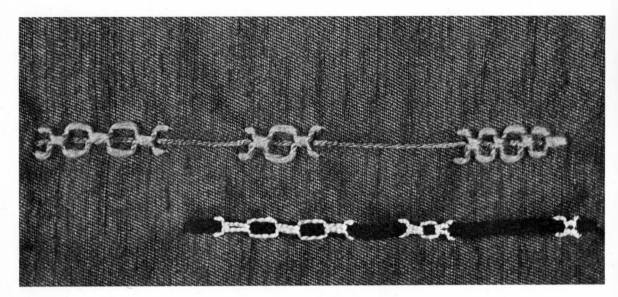

Lock stitch worked in two differing thread weights

# Couching with canvas stitches

As the aim of canvas stitchery is to cover the canvas ground, it would be inappropriate to the discipline to lay threads directly onto the canvas ground. However, after the surface of the canvas has been covered in simple stitches, then couched threads can be added on top.

The couching stitches should be chosen with care; they should not obscure too much of the ground stitches. Upright Gobelin, either spaced or clustered, is unobtrusive, as is the slanting Encroaching Gobelin over thick threads. Tent stitch also merges well into the background and is an excellent stitch for couching over curved lines. Spaced Cross stitch, Double Cross stitch and Florentine could be used on straight line couching but their heavy effect could alter the character of the work if used indiscriminately. Holbein is an outline stitch found in canvas work but it may be used for a flexible line of couching in itself over a ground of other stitches.

The nature of canvas work offers scope in the use of counterchange both in the colour of the ground and in the couched and couching threads.

Fine silk thread couched onto canvas work background

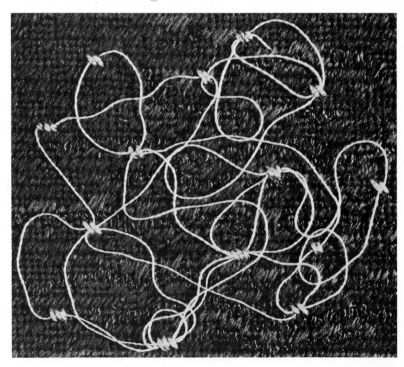

Raffene and thick wools couched by sewing machine using straight and zigzag stitch onto canvas work background

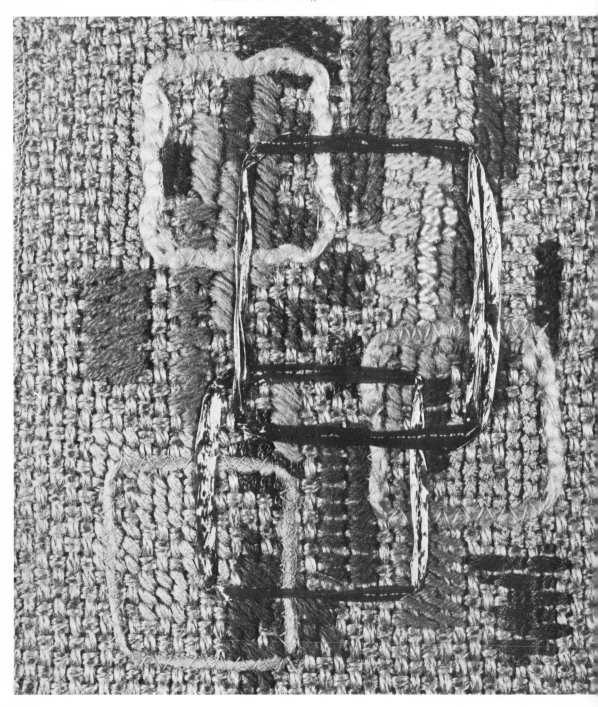

Raffene, wools, perle and stranded silk
couched onto canvas work background
by Spaced Cross Stitch, Florentine, Upright
and Encroaching Gobelin and Tent stitch

# Couching with beads and sequins

Beads and Sequins have to be used with care as a method of couching as their shiny nature detracts from the actual thread to be couched down. They look well as an integral part of a motif as bead flowers with a stem of couched thread, for instance.

Beads are often difficult to place precisely, especially round ones. The couching thread may be taken through the beads and invisible couching stitches added to hold them in place. Another exciting effect may be achieved by twisting a string of beads round the couched thread before it is couched down.

Shiny beads and sequins should generally be used on rich-looking fabrics, but thickly textured fabrics such as wool tweeds and hopsack offer interesting possibilities of contrast.

Couching can be used to hold down paillettes and similar large decorations; an interesting texture results from needle-weaving over the couched threads.

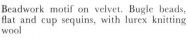

Beadwork motif on velvet. Bugle beads, flat and cup sequins, with lurex knitting wool

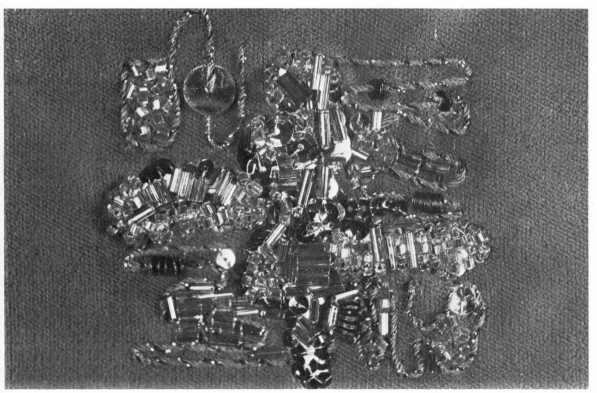

Beadwork motif for evening purse. Lurex, perlita and raffene couched by chain, open chain, detached chain, zigzag chain and straight stitch

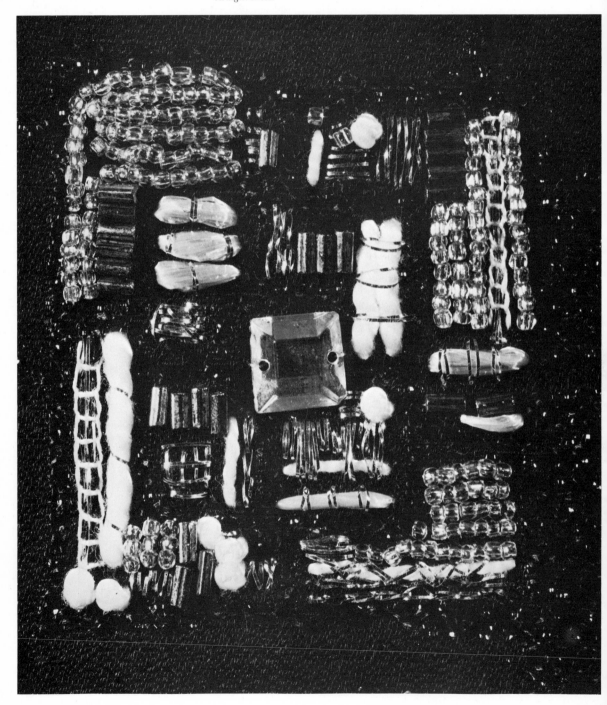

Grey beads with grey perle chain stitch on
wool fabric

Green pearls and green glass bead on
openweave fabric from which threads
have been drawn and replaced with wool

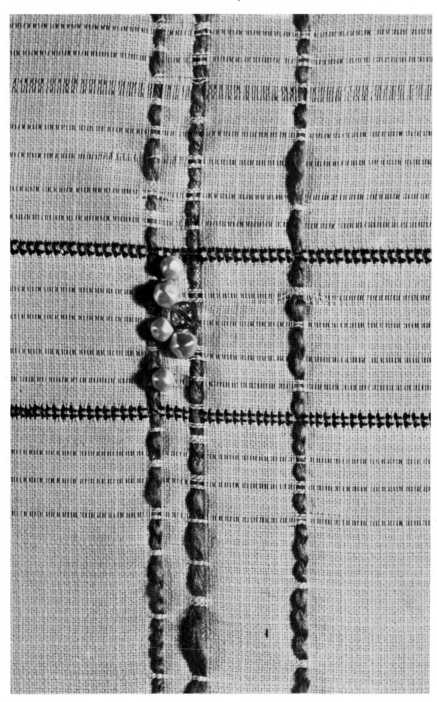

# Couching with the sewing machine

The sewing machine affords a quick means of couching large areas as well as producing original effects of its own. Machine couching is especially suitable for items which may need frequent laundering. Conversely it is capable of delicate and interesting textures.

The straight stitch on the machine can be used with the presser foot, or cording foot, to couch threads down the centre. The choice of couched thread is important as the presser foot tends to flatten it and the straight stitch itself may distort the thread. Loosen the top tension if a hard line persists. By removing the foot and by either lowering the feed teeth or covering them with a special plate, much more flexibility can be achieved.

Satin stitch in blocks or spots is effective, though trouble may be encountered with a very hairy thread as the fluff tends to cling to the shuttle race mechanism.

Machine couching using Running stitch (left to right): running stitch down centre of knitting wool, perlita and raffene; to one side only of weaving yarn

Machine couching using blind stitch (left to right): blind stitch on normal setting; at its widest on two different weaving yarns and one knitting wool

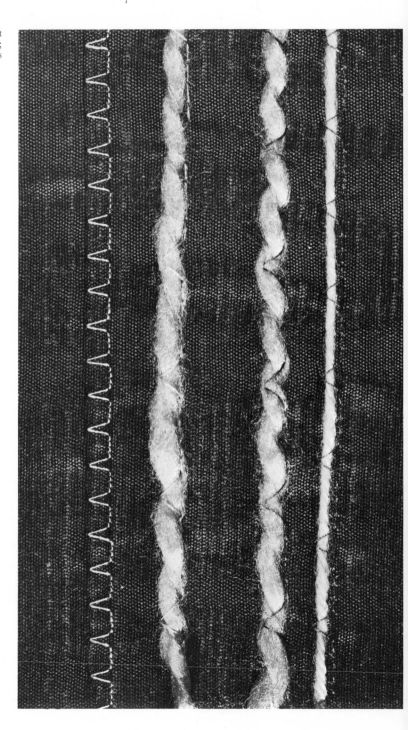

Detail from colour plate 3

The perle was worked from the back on straight stitch by winding it onto a bobbin. The tension screw mechanism was removed from the bobbin case and the presser foot removed and feed teeth lowered. The wool was worked from the front with a loose zigzag (settings 2 to 4) with the satin stitch spots at the corners. Beads were added by hand

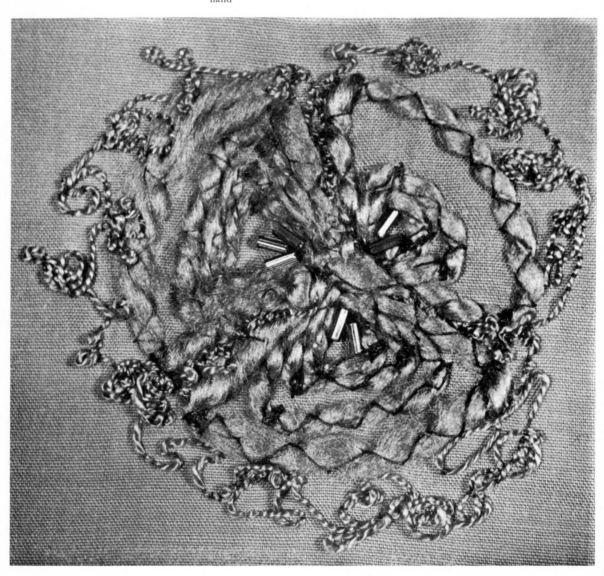

Straight stitch couching floss silk shapes
around machined cutwork centre

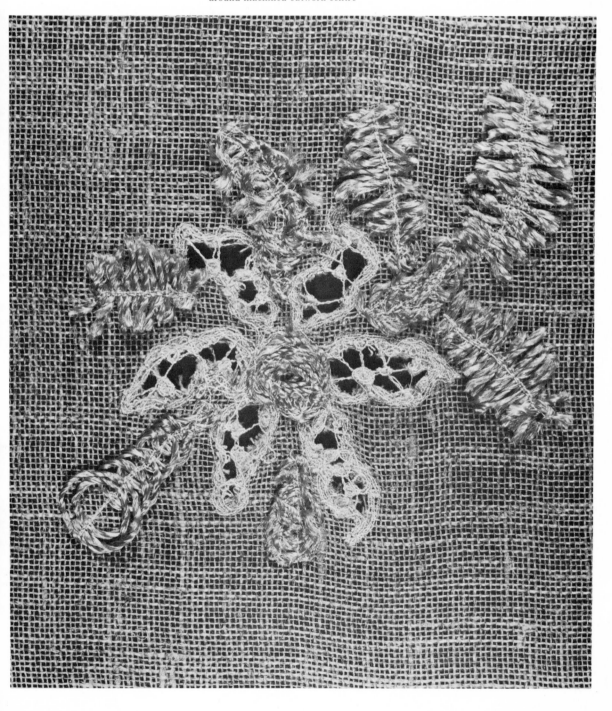

Straight stitch couching large area of filoselle freely laid down

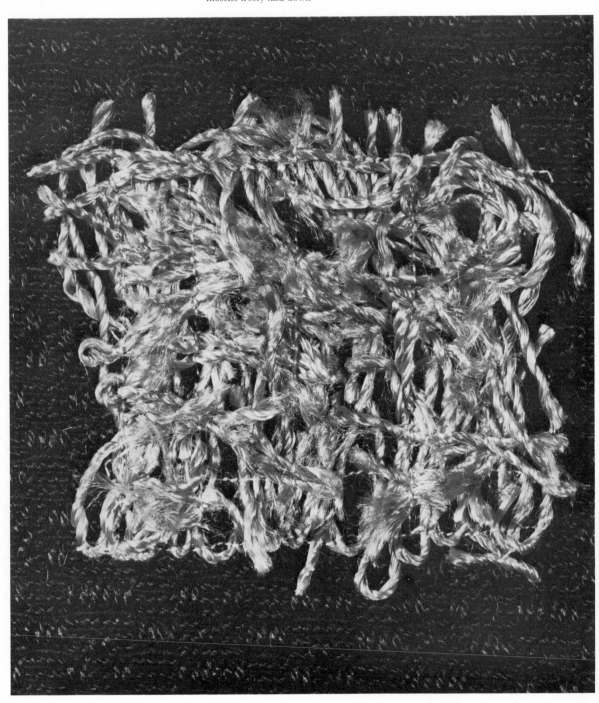

Batik fabric background, machine embroidered with cellular design. Shapes are emphasized by couched wool, which was machined down the centre with straight stitch

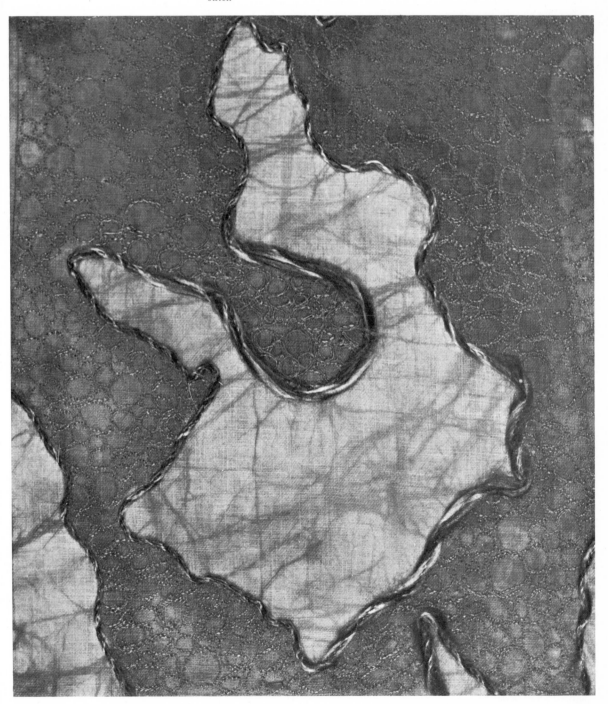

String machined down with zigzag stitch

The zigzag stitch is useful on firm threads but needs to be fairly loose as it tends to flatten the couched thread or cause it to cluster; variation of the stitch length and width counteracts a too regular effect. A feature can be made of the zigzag itself by using a contrasting thread in the needle.

Other automatic stitches may be used for couching, depending on the type and flexibility of the sewing machine available.

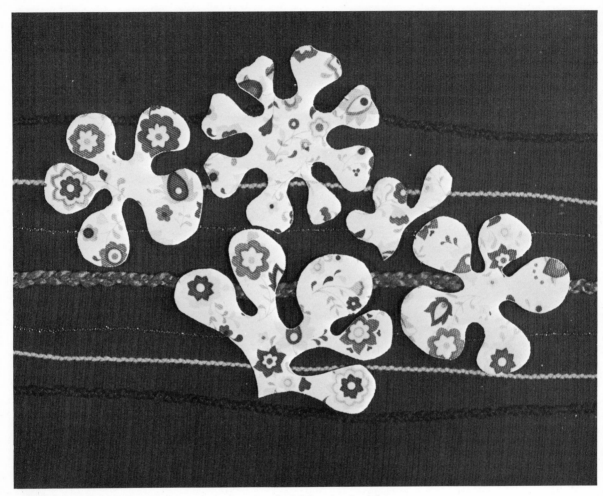

By winding a thick thread onto the bobbin and either loosening the tension spring or removing the entire spring and screw mechanism altogether from the bobbin case, the thick thread can be couched down by a thin top thread in the machine. This technique is worked from the back of the fabric and needs to be tightly framed.

By removing the presser foot and lowering the feed teeth mechanism a much freer texture results.

Machine couching using silver crochet twist
and lurex thread

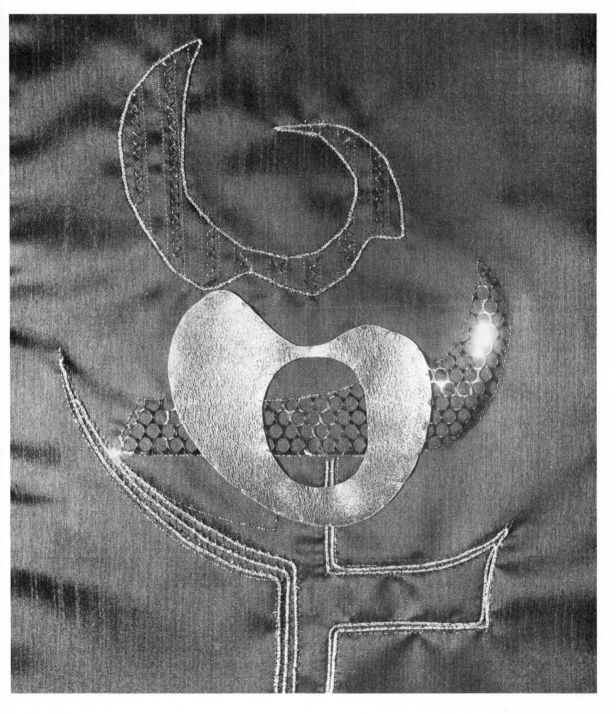

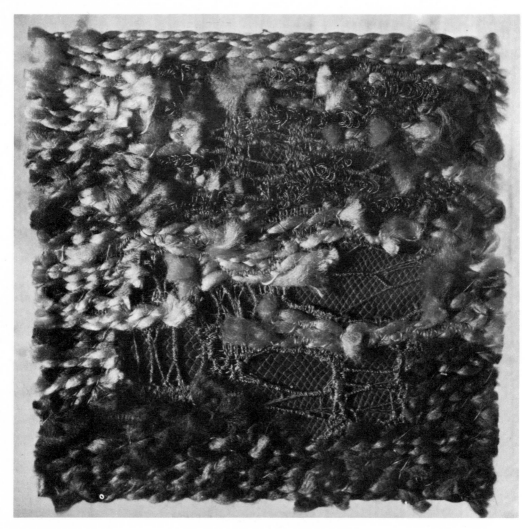

Pulled work done on the sewing machine;
the wools are couched both by hand and by
the sewing machine, using zigzag stitch to
give textural variation

# Bibliography

Barbara Dawson    *Metal Thread Embroidery*
B. T. Batsford (1976)

Betty Chicken    *Introducing Design in Embroidery*
B. T. Batsford (1971)

Diana Springall    *Canvas Embroidery*
B. T. Batsford (1971)

M. Thomas    *Dictionary of Embroidery Stitches*
Hodder and Stoughton (19th edition 1974)

Kathleen Whyte    *Design in Embroidery*
B. T. Batsford (1970)

Constance Howard    *Inspiration for Embroidery*
B. T. Batsford (1967)

# Suppliers

**GREAT BRITAIN**

## Threads, fabrics and embroidery accessories

*Art Needlework Industries Limited*
7 St Michael's Mansions,
Ship Street, Oxford

*Dryad Limited*
Northgate, Leicester

*Hugh Griffiths*
Brookdale
8 Frome Road, Beckington,
Bath BA3 6TD
(Weaving yarns)

*Mace and Nairn*
89 Crane Street, Salisbury, Wilts

*The Needlewoman Shop*
146 Regent Street, London W1

*Elizabeth Tracy*
Pathfields House, 45 High Street,
Haslemere, Surrey
(Embroidery materials)

# Suppliers

**USA**

## Threads and embroidery accessories

*American Thread Corporation*
90 Park Avenue, New York

*Appleton Brothers of London*
West Main Road, Little Compton
Rhode Island 02837

*Bucky King Embroideries*
Unlimited 121 South Drive
Pittsburgh, Pennsylvania 15238

*The Needle's Point Studio*
7013 Duncraig Court,
McLean, Virginia 22101

*The Rusty Needle*
1479 Glenneyre,
Laguna Beach, California 92651

*Joan Toggitt*
1170 Broadway, New York
N Y 10001

*Yarn Depot*
545 Sutter Street
San Francisco 95102